Information Gone Almost-Wild

Yet We're Still
So Under-Informed

— we just need a little more information about you for our files,
... for your convenience —

INFORMATION GONE ALMOST-WILD

(An Information Age Manifesto)

JOHN DALSTON

(Under-Informed Over-Simplifier)

INFORMATION GONE ALMOST-WILD

Edition 1.0

Copyright © 2011 by John Dalston

All rights reserved. No part of this book may be reproduced in any form by any electronic or mechanical means (including photocopying, recording, or information storage and retrieval) without permission in writing from the publisher.

Published on Earth, in the United States of America
by AspectEdge, LLC., Florida.
www.AspectEdge.com

ISBN 978-0-9819579-1-3 (trade paperback)

Almost-dedicated to the idea that YOU should be better informed,
 . . . for my convenience.

Introduction

Once upon a time there was no Information Age, and we had to put up with just being industrious, and growing the flora and the fauna; which was a pity, but back then they didn't know what conveniences they were missing.

Once upon a time we were all *less*-informed, and in the future we hope to be *more*-informed. For now, we are just barely almost-informed, and sometimes agonizingly under-informed.

Most of what we call "life" consists of becoming informed, processing information, and informing others; and each of our too-short, trying quests is at best only almost-complete with imaginings, surprises, and learning experiences that range in nature from the tranquil to the wild.

About the Information Age

Just like with previous ages, the thing central to the age (information, in this case, as opposed to industry or agriculture) has been around . . . for ages. As with the other ages, when the Information Age ceases to preside, it is still expected to continue, and evolve.

While other ages were dominating, information morphed into its chronicled form with the introduction of "permanent" memory (cave paintings, paper, and books). Then came the era of instant communication (electricity, and the telegraph). What brought the age into nearly full bloom was the introduction of computer networks—adding more speed, memory, accurate processing, and establishing a global brain-like architecture. Looking back, we can see that it was information that has fueled change and progress.

About "Information Gone Almost-Wild"

The use of the word "wild" in the title is meant to include both the almost-negative and the almost-positive connotations: entangled, atavistic, immoral, and unrestrained, as well as fast, interesting, vigorous, and generative.

The use of the word "almost" in the title is meant to convey that there is constant review and restraint within the system, as well as a much flirting with danger, experimentation, and reaching.

As with anything double-edged, we must be careful how we use information. We have a way of testing presumed limits, teetering on the untried, settling back to a more mature position, and then testing different limits, . . . and so on.

About Being "Under-Informed"

Almost everyone is at the same time reasonably-confident *and* quite humble about what they think they mostly know, because they know they don't know everything. There is a general expectation that knowing more would be better. We ask questions. We learn and experiment so that we can compete and succeed. In science, we hold onto the best model that explains things, until an even better model comes along. We have established the legal burden of proof thresholds of "preponderance of the evidence," "clear and convincing evidence," and "beyond a reasonable doubt" to judiciously avoid the almost-impossible hurdle "beyond the shadow of a doubt." In the court of public opinion and in everyday life we label things as "dubious," "uncertain," or "controversial" until things are better explained.

More after these messages . . . .

About Being a Manifesto

This is a manifesto about the current state of our world with respect to the Information Age generally. Unlike some manifestos, this one is not in support of a particular agenda (other than that of advancing information awareness and encouraging debate on the various issues). It covers many topics, but doesn't go into any one deeply. Just about everyone is in an information-related occupation now, even those in mining, farming, and fishing. This manifesto is meant for everyone interested in the Information Age.

I have tried to concentrate on the competing values and trends, and also on the seeming and real contradictions that are at play. This is a book about the tensions and dynamics of our age.

There are some things that are diametrically opposed, and then many more that are just somewhat contradictory. In *The Almost-Dictionary*, I described the term "almost-opposite" to mean something that does not fully neutralize or cancel something out when they are brought together. While "left" and "right" can be considered opposites; "organic" and "inorganic," and "capitalist" and "socialist," might better be considered almost-opposites (as might alternative alleles of the same gene). The "almost" is often in the details. Also, often, things work in synergy *to some degree*.

There is some speculation about the near-future at the end, given current trends. (In the future, comparing the future here with the future there may be of interest.)

About Things Being "For Your Convenience"

I do try to point out how convenient things have become — the result of that promise that came with connectivity, electricity, electronics, computerization, and then the Internet, and that continues with the introduction of new gadgets and applications that are designed to improve our lives.

Generally speaking, what is done is usually done for someone's convenience. People may benefit directly or indirectly. Something that might *not* be in your interest now, might *eventually* be in your interest (like studying, or filing information in a tidy manner). Sometimes you only get the benefit of something that is in your interest if you are aware that it is there, recognize that it is in your interest, and take action. At other times, other people are busy doing things that are in your interest and you will never know.

There are many possibilities that might be convenient if things were made simpler and easier, and so many people find

Information Gone Almost-Wild

themselves employed trying to facilitate and add conveniences almost everywhere.

In an Information Age, you are definitely going to find information convenient, and helpful, and it is my hope that you will find the information presented here to be just of that type.

About the Minimalist Style

For you convenience, there is much information that is *not* included here. Please consult other books for a review of the Information Age in historical context—the players and events. There are other books that focus only on subparts of the Information Age. There are other books that focus on the economy, and discuss possible business solutions and opportunities. There are many sources that chronicle abuses of information or access. There are anecdotes in many books that serve to make them almost-repetitious. You are spared all that here.

Also, everything but the main points have been almost-omitted (never written) for brevity—which you might appreciate as you try to fit reading this book into your busy day. (This is another "almost-book.")

About How to Read this Book

Most books are read in a plain or normal voice, but this book might most appropriately be read in your advertising "smiley voice." (Alternatively, you could only almost-read this by getting someone else to read it to you in *their* advertising smiley voice.)

Information Gone Almost-Wild

This book has been modified from its almost-original version (previous draft). It has been formatted to fit inside the cover and edited to be readable in the time allotted and for content.

Information Gone Almost-Wild

This page was intentionally left almost-blank.

Contents

Introduction i
Mostly Basics 1
Almost Obviously 23
Almost-Secure 55
Almost-Enough 79
Almost-News 95
Almost-Healthy 105
Mostly Helpful 113
Almost-War 135
Almost-There 147
Almost-Somebody 175
Almost-Concluded 195
Appendices 199

Information Gone Almost-Wild

This is another almost-blank page, basically.

Mostly Basics

A specter is razzle-dazzling the people of the world — the specter of information. The powers of the world have to varying degrees entered into a mostly-tacit alliance to welcome the information that is already almost everywhere, ... for everyone's convenience.

Information is attractive.
The more information the better.
The faster information moves the better.
The more current the information the better.
The more accurate the information the better.
The more succinct the information the better.
The more specific the information the better.
The more reliable the information the better.
The more organized the information the better.
The more ubiquitous the information the better.
The more meta-information the better.

Information can move at or near the speed of light, so change can happen quickly, ... for your convenience.

If you blink, you'll miss it.

Everyone and everything is interconnected.

What we see is individuality everywhere.

In the Information Age,
information is everyone's
most-prized possession.

In the Information Age,
everyone is trying their hardest
to make sure you are never
the very *last* person to know,
... for your convenience.

> The way to reform any process is with *more* and *better* information, ... for everyone's convenience.

The more people, the more agendas.

The more people, the more groups.
The more groups, the more agendas.

The more groups, the more groups of groups.
The more groups of groups,
the more agendas.

We're all in the same
boat together.

Nobody is against the system,
but everybody wants to change it,
... for their and your convenience.

A diversity of opinions is good,
as long as we submit to groupthink.

Groupthink is good,
as long as we maintain a
diversity of opinions.

The ability to update information in many places around the world simultaneously and quickly is bound to be indispensable.

The ability to update information in many places around the world simultaneously and quickly is bound to prove problematic.

The direction of the Information Age
may be summed up in the single phrase:
Abolition of private information.

Nothing has changed really,
public information is still public,
and private information is still "public to
some degree, depending on some kind
of a need-to-know,"
... which is to say "almost-private."

On the Internet,
all animals are equal,
but some animals are
more equal than others,
. . . for their convenience,
. . . for your convenience.

Information is here to stay.
You may accidentally "delete" some of it,
but we have backups,
. . . for your convenience.

Mostly Basics

> The hope is that increased openness,
> accessibility, transparency, surveillance,
> disclosure requirements, and oversight,
> will have the overall effect
> of *deterring* bad behavior
> and *encouraging* good behavior,
> . . . for your convenience.

Information Gone Almost-Wild

A circumspect guardedness allows you
to protect your reputation and maintain
a competitive advantage.

Being transparent allows others
to see your trustworthiness, your value,
and your strengths.

The longer you keep information
to yourself,
the longer you get to make use
of that superior knowledge.

The longer you keep information
to yourself,
the more the world is going to
move around you and leave you
behind. (Use it, or lose it.)

> In the Information Age,
> you are a "sitting duck"
> to everyone else,
> just as everyone else
> is a "sitting duck" to you,
> ... for your convenience.

> In the Information Age,
> everyone knows where your
> children go to school, comrade,
> . . . for your convenience.

> You can learn more than any teacher
> knows just by browsing the Internet,
> . . . for your convenience.

To err is human.

With a computer, you can really foul things up.

But with an Internet,
things just keep getting better and better,
... for your convenience.

The best way to explore space
is to send information-gathering
probes out there,

to send information back here,

. . . for your convenience.

The reason we're looking for
space aliens is that we need
information about them for our files,
. . . for your convenience.

Information Gone Almost-Wild

This page is obviously almost-blank.

Almost Obviously

Information Gone Almost-Wild

The more we all both compete *and* cooperate the better. Partnering brings with it both leverage and interdependence.
Sharing brings openness, comparisons, and friendship.
Competition brings out the best in all of us,
. . . for everyone's convenience.

Almost Obviously

As nations become more partners
than competitors,
and as organizations become more
partners than competitors,
and particularly as transportation,
communications, and everything
speeds up, the less there will be
a distinction between "us" and "them,"
. . . for everyone's convenience.

A world of white hats and black hats,
has been replaced by a world of gray hats,
hats that alternate white and black,
checkered hats, hat swapping, transparent
hats, secret alternate hats, multiple hats,
paper-thin hats, hat fashions, moths,
helmets, umbrellas, and bald good looks.

They say the things that "move mountains"
are fear, greed, crisis, and law,
all of which involve *new* information,
. . . for your convenience.

Mountains of information
can now be moved
with the click of a button,
. . . for your convenience.

The only fair way is for
everyone to get information
all at the same time,
. . . for everyone's convenience.

If everybody finds out the same
information at the same time,
"analysis paralysis" kicks in,
. . . for everyone's entertainment.

We don't want your opinions,
because we already know all the facts,
. . . for our convenience,
. . . for your convenience.

We have this brief questionnaire for
you to fill out,
and we very much appreciate you
calling in to our show to let us know
what you think,
. . . for our convenience,
. . . for your convenience.

The easiest way to suppress
information is to not create it,
the next easiest way is to bury it and
not talk about it,
and we'd tell you the third easiest way
but there needs to be more study done
on this first,
. . . for your convenience.

One way for a company to remain competitive is to NOT share the information it has.

Another way is for the company to trade the information it has
for information it doesn't have,
... until it has all the information available,
... for its convenience,
... for your convenience.

Almost Obviously

Information sharing presents huge risks.

Of course, these risks will be mitigated effectively and securely in a timely fashion, with the appropriate respect for the sensitivity and value of the information, ... for your convenience.

Information can fit in anywhere, and databases can be built to an extent and complexity without limit.

The great thing about information is that once collected it may be applied for so many different and even unforeseen purposes,
. . . for your convenience.

If you haven't started hoarding information on everyone on the planet yet, there are thousands of companies out there that can help you get started,
. . . for your convenience.

Almost Obviously

> Whoever has the largest database ... **wins**,
> ... for your convenience.

An age based upon something that
seems determined to be free
probably won't last very long.

The cheaper a commodity the more it will be
used; and if it is information, the more
innovation and learning is likely to take place.

Information about events, discoveries, people, and new ideas are produced in an endless steady stream, so unlike an economy built on land, gold, or other limited resource, the Information Age economy could last indefinitely, ... for your convenience.

Information Gone Almost-Wild

In the Information Age, you don't need
to keep track of anything,
because the tracking is all being done
for you,
. . . for your convenience.

We need those status updates from
you ever more frequently,
with more and more detail please,
. . . for our convenience,
. . . for your convenience.

> Backup systems that don't involve electronics and software are becoming impractical, obsolete, and unusable.

> What good is a backup system that can't replace the "production" system!

Information Gone Almost-Wild

When someone deletes (or anonymizes) their copy of your information,
that doesn't *necessarily* mean that a different copy doesn't exist somewhere else
(for audit, quality, or evidentiary purposes),
... for their convenience,
... for your convenience.

The more used-and-then-discarded information storage devices there are, the more opportunity for you to discover what your competition is doing,
... for your convenience.

It took about ten years to go from:
WYSIWYG (What You See Is What You Get),
to: WYSI-HA-HA (What You See Is What
We See You See),
and WAKY (We Almost-Know You),
. . . for your convenience.

Transparency only allows us to
help you more-efficiently,
. . . for your convenience.

The game of "cat and mouse" between
employer and employee, government and
individual, insurer and insured,
spouse and spouse, parent and child,
is getting a whole lot easier for the cats,
... for their convenience.

Tracking loved ones, feared ones,
and interesting ones, and predicting where
people are going to be next,
are just a few of the services we offer,
... for your convenience.

Almost Obviously

Almost-Travel, *v., n.* The next best thing to being there. Your almost-trip can start sooner, is over faster, and you don't need as many suitcases. When you think media and technology, think almost-travel. Almost-travel is almost-always good enough.
- from *The Almost-Dictionary.*

We have phones, television, teleconferencing, and the Internet. We now have indoor snow skiing in warm places, and tanning salons in cold places. We even have remote-surgery. More and more, real travel is becoming a waste of time,
and less and less convenient.

The automobile used to be
a "horseless carriage,"
and then a "freedom machine,"
but now it is a "bucket of gadgets,"
and a "networked device,"
that just happens to come with some
necessary old-fashioned
environmentally-unfriendly
contraption that is hidden in that place
prescribed by the ancient ones (and that
can only be serviced where they have
other gadgets that can talk to those
gadgets),
. . . for your convenience.

Almost Obviously

The Driver's License was introduced because people lacked information on how to safely operate a vehicle; but now the problem is almost the reverse, and an overabundance of information is vying for the attention of the too-often "distracted" driver, ... for their convenience.

(The Driver's License itself is now *only* used to get other information.)

The tagging of **things** is bound to put thieves out of business, and make finding everything easy, even from great distances (maybe even if the things are not yours), and it will eliminate extra steps from many industrial and business processes, and add precision to the identification of whatever you encounter,
. . . for your convenience.

There is a place for everything, and everything stationary will be asking everything with a carrying capacity to please help it get to its right place,
. . . for your convenience.

Almost Obviously

> Taking things apart and creating new things from the tagged components is going to make for some interesting . . . conversations, . . . for your convenience.

Information Gone Almost-Wild

> The number and types of things that can move at or near the speed of light is increasing rapidly: light, electricity, telegraph messages, phone calls, radio shows, television broadcasts, money, transaction records, software, pictures, music, tax records, medical records, remote control information, newspapers, books, movies, and now 3D movies,
> ... for your convenience.

There is nothing that can elude,
leak, age, become forgotten, or
altered, and slip through the
cracks faster than information,
. . . for your convenience.

Problems make the world go 'round,
because fixing problems is how we all
get paid,
. . . for everyone's convenience.

What we need are solutions, and with
them quality, durability, and reliability,
. . . for everyone's convenience.

> The more problems, the more jobs.
>
> The more people, the more problems.

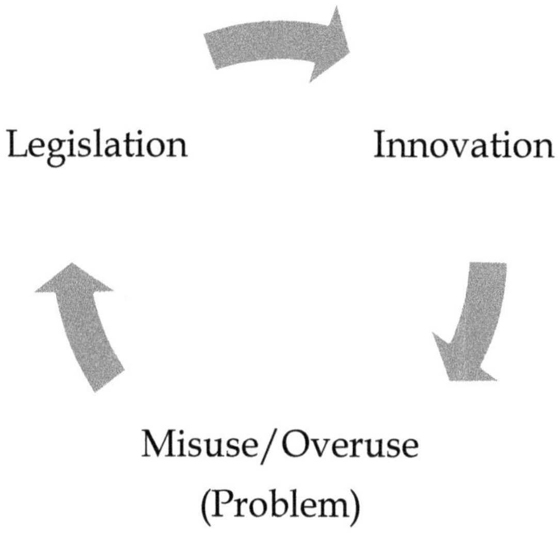

Legislation   Innovation

Misuse/Overuse
(Problem)

Fig. 2.1 An almost-vicious yet almost-perfect almost-cycle.

> If you're not part of the problem,
> you're part of the solution.

Solving every problem with the solution of
"more, better, and faster information" might
itself become a problem,
. . . for everyone's convenience.

Almost Obviously

We all get to deal with
"information overload" in our own way.

For any technology company this presents
endless opportunities for developing new
and better products
and simple-to-use services,
as ways for people to unwind and relax,
... for their convenience,
... for your convenience.

Thankfully, also, the ubiquitous
dumpster is there when you need it,
... for your convenience.

Everyone must be a specialist.

You can't know everything,
but you can compete if you focus,
. . . for your own sanity and convenience.

Everyone must be a generalist.

You can't afford to say no to new ideas
just because they emerged first in
other fields.

Doing anything
without first notifying everyone else
has become almost-impossible.

It's becoming easier and easier to
just do-it-yourself.

> Individuals can now do what, until recently, only groups could do; but that just makes groups more powerful than they ever were.

3

Almost-Secure

Sometimes the best way to protect your information is to make as many backup copies of it as possible, and to let some company safely archive it for you, and to send a copy to the government (so you can prove that it's yours later), and to publish it (so everyone knows that it's yours), and to repeat it every chance you get (so nobody forgets that it's yours), . . . for your convenience.

Information and knowledge are a
public good,
... even though a little bit of the
wrong information and knowledge in
the wrong hands (heads) could mean
disaster for everyone.

The path of least resistance
for information is sometimes
to go almost everywhere at once,
... for your convenience.

Information Gone Almost-Wild

The safest way to present yourself in
"social networking" situations is to:
divulge as little true information about
yourself as possible,
post no pictures,
include no links,
befriend no one,
search for nobody, and nothing,
turn all of the privacy settings that until
now you didn't know you had to "stun,"
delete all your Internet accounts,
destroy all your gadgets,
and live like a hermit off the grid,
. . . for your inconvenience,
. . . for your convenience.

Never before have so many
divulged so much about themselves,
so freely,
to so many strangers,
for so long,
with so few safeguards,
and so few overarching systemic
controls,
and with so little
personal incentive to do so.

If you have nothing to fear,
you have nothing to hide.

The way to prevent identity theft
and other misuses of information
is to minimize access to
information everywhere about
everyone,
. . . for everyone's convenience.

Everyone must add or update
information about others
as part of their job,
. . . for everyone's convenience.

Almost-Secure

You are the one ultimately responsible for keeping your sensitive personal information secure and private, ("don't let yourself become a victim"), even if it is the information that you don't have any control over that is the information that needs to be secure and private,
. . . for your convenience.

Identity theft has been the "fastest growing" crime for so long that television commercials joke about it. You too will be laughing once you are able to tag and follow your imposters real-time, for sport and entertainment,
. . . and for your convenience.

> Information sharing: the cause of, and solution to, all of the world's problems.

> If the worst thing, economically speaking, would be to apply the brakes to information sharing, then the best thing might be to accelerate information sharing. No company wants to compete with anyone armed with more and better information. Therefore, the microeconomic *and* macroeconomic inclination is for the formation of ever-larger potential and actual victims of cyber attacks and other information-related crimes.

> The more things that are "hackable," the more hacking there will be.

There will always be more dots to connect. The dots will always need to be connected faster. There will always be a need to connect more dots automatically. Self-connecting dots would be almost-ideal.

You can't analyze *any* of the information you don't collect.

The Information Age rests upon a foundations of trust, fear, confidence, and hope. We trust the authorities, our institutions, and our technology. We rely on the fear associated with penalties. The economy depends on business confidence, lender confidence, and consumer confidence. And hope drives positive action.

We can only ever be *mostly* trusting, fearful, confident, and hopeful; and still, all of these things may be undermined in an instant.

Your most compromising employee
is still on your payroll
(in the same way that your tallest
employee is still on your payroll).

It might not be your job to investigate
and monitor your coworkers, but
someone near you has some due
diligence in that regard,
. . . for your convenience.

Information Gone Almost-Wild

> The more accounts and passwords you have the better (the more important you become), ... for your convenience.

> Security access traditionally involves some combination of the following: something you know, something you have, and something about you. The trend is for *more* information to transfer with each: *stronger* passwords, *smarter* cards, and *fuller* body scans. So expect password fatigue, and, more-generally, authentication fatigue syndrome (AFS) to continue until everything around you thinks it knows who you are, ... for your convenience.

Almost-Secure

Our Information Security and
Information Privacy policies are
prominently displayed at all times,
. . . for your convenience.

We must reserve the right to revise our
Information Security and Information
Privacy policies at any time,
. . . for your convenience.

The Almost-Expected Company Credo:

- Information security is our greatest concern.
- The privacy and confidentiality of personal information must be maintained.
- Protecting our intellectual property is our highest concern.
- Guarding our corporate secrets is our most pressing need.
- Protecting national security interests is essential.
- Information transparency and openness is our prime objective.
- Speed is critical for success.
- Quality is the name of the game.
- Maintaining standards of safety and excellent is of utmost importance.
- Communicating effectively with our partners and regulators is vital.
- Managing risk is the key ingredient.
- Being both mature and nimble is crucial.
- Ensuring that we hire the right people is the most important thing.
- The safety of our employees is our #1 priority.
- The profits of our shareholders is primary.
- Growing and increasing market-share is how we keep moving forward.
- Supply-chain management is an imperative.
- Outsourcing allows us to concentrate on our core competencies.
- We do all of the above while protecting the environment, and giving back to our communities.
- And, of course, everything we do is for our customer's convenience.

The Almost-Expected "Stretch for Excellence":

- Therefore, we have put processes and procedures in place to make sure shit like this never happens again.

Databases are designed to both protect
and reveal information,
. . . for your convenience.

(So by definition, databases are at best
only almost-secure.)

Database owners only almost-own the
personal information they hold,
because of the other stakeholders,
and the people the information is about.

Database controllers only mostly-control
the personal information in the database,
because of all the others exerting control
over the information,
. . . for your convenience.

Since the Internet began, there have been
and are many powers at play: some want
certain things and ways
to be more secure,
and some want certain things and ways to
be more open,
. . . for their convenience,
. . . and for everyone's convenience.

There is no such thing as complete security,
so the Internet just keeps taking
"almost-secure"
to never-before-seen levels of almost-secure,
. . . for your convenience.

Sometimes it's nice to have choices:

First you build it, then you make it safe and secure.

First you design it to be secure, safe, and to fail safe, and then you build it.

First you never stop designing and building it to be only almost-secure.

The tendency is for systems to increase in
functionality and grow in complexity.

Complexity
is one of the chief enemies of security.

Things that can move virally often do;
of course, over the distribution channels
that the Big Partners control,
. . . for your safety, entertainment, and
convenience.

Intellectual property is only "property" when it is treated as such.

No one knows all the laws — that body of information is just too vast.

Laws keep changing.

Not all laws are enforced all the time.

The best security defense is achieved by making the various and often disjointed components of the fortress *appear* impenetrable and imponderable, while it continues to evolve.

Everyone has a weakness.

There is always a way.

Information Gone Almost-Wild

Once upon a time they lived happily ever after.

Almost-Enough

We have never known more, yet we are still desperate for more information about the very small picture, and the very big picture.

We use words, in "physics," as stand-ins for what we only almost-know: "matter," "energy," "wave," "quark," "time," "space," "everything."

There are "gold nuggets" of information even in the mundane and everyday things, and we are on the edge of our seats waiting for the next new insight.

If you wait five minutes,
even better information will come along,
. . . for your convenience.

Not acting now (with only the
information you have)
can be disastrous.

Not knowing enough
can be a dangerous thing.

Knowing too much
can be a dangerous thing.

There is nothing more helpful
than being interrupted with the right
information at the right time,
and this needs to happen
as often as possible,
... for your convenience.

There is nothing worse
than being interrupted with
unwanted information
at just the wrong time,
and this needs to happen
as little as possible,
... for your convenience.

People only ever almost-understand what someone says (you can only "read between the lines" to some degree), and what is said is only close to what is meant (due to the limitations of the language and the vagueness in words).

* * *

People only ever almost-understand what is almost-meant.

Gossip is almost-currency.

There are at least three sides
to every story: yours, theirs,
and what really happened.

History is hard to know, because
everyone tells it like it almost was.

In each situation there are
two types of people:
those who don't know enough to make the
best decision (non-experts),
and those who vehemently disagree with
each other (experts),
so somebody just needs to put their foot
down (decide, and hope for the best),
... for their convenience,
... for your convenience.

Or not.

They already know almost everything about you; therefore, you may as well comply with their next request for more information about you for their files,
. . . for your convenience.

Those you *don't* want to find out, will (because you are on their radar).
And those you *do* want to find out, won't (because they have their filters on),
. . . for their convenience.

Information Gone Almost-Wild

Original: The filters are getting better and better at keeping the bomb-designs and kiddy-porn scarce,
and who knows what else,
... for your convenience.

Revision 1: The filters are getting better and better at keeping the ▬▬▬▬
and ▬▬▬ scarce,
and ▬▬▬▬▬▬ ,
... for your convenience.

Revision 2: The filters are getting better,
... for your convenience.

Revision 3: The filters are designed to produce almost-pure goodness,
... for your convenience.

Whoever controls the filters can make you feel as secure as they think you want to feel,
. . . for your convenience,
. . . for their convenience,
. . . for your convenience.

Perception trumps reality,
. . . until reality trumps perception.

> There is more going on behind the scenes than you can possibly imagine.

> Most information will just bore you to tears.

Obsolete ideas often linger,
so it is up to everyone to seek out the best
ideas and to stay current,
. . . for everyone's convenience.

I'm ok, *and* you're ok.

Even though information is trying to be
free, there are still those tactful enough
to withhold information when necessary,
varnish the truth,
candy-coat the problem,
or do everything they can to evade,
obfuscate, mislead, misfollow,
bedazzle, delay, and quibble,
so that information does not
unnecessarily go awry,
. . . for your convenience.

The best way to make discoveries — by
solving the maze, peeling the onion,
finding the needle in the haystack, or
surmounting the wall of difficulty — is
with new information,
. . . for your convenience.

Curiosity may sometimes kill the cat,
but usually the cat just has a
"learning experience."
(Or the cat just stops laughing, and
catches his breath.)

Information Gone Almost-Wild

This page is as almost-blank as it always was.

Almost-News

Information Gone Almost-Wild

Why watch the way-too-much-detail news, research the we-hide-it-and-you-go-seek-it news, and wait around for the you-get-it-when-we-want-to-give-it-to-you news, when right now you can watch the humorous news, entertainment news, dirt, spin, fluff, sports news, and calamity-only news,
... for your convenience.

Almost-news is usually *better* than "real news."

Don't publicize your negative news,
because that could work against you.
And don't publicize your positive news,
because copycats will copy you
and steal market-share.
Still, you do need to blow your own horn,
. . . about something.

The best way to think of the
advertising you see,
is that it is almost-news,
. . . and *for* your convenience,
. . . for your convenience.

The best way to think about your favorite
songs being used in advertising, is that
you get to hear your favorite songs again,
. . . for your convenience.

(A win-win-win-win-win for musician,
advertiser, shopkeeper, shopper, and
discerning music lover.)

A unique personalized, filtered, and customized blend of newsadspinertainment, (news, advertising, spin, and entertainment) should bring you all of the information you want, and none of the information you don't want,
. . . for your convenience.

Personalized newsadspinertainment will only spur the need for new apps—that will help you find out what it is that other people know.

The end-products of creativity are
now easy-to-copy files,
instead of difficult-to-copy things
(records, tapes, newspapers, books,
paintings, films, etc.), and the
transition can be likened to going
off the "gold standard"
to a reliance on "market forces,"
which helps keep prices down,
. . . for your convenience.

Digital information is better,
simply because it is exact.

Almost-News

> Since information (and therefore files) want to be free, this inadvertent but fortuitous "liberating" of the creative urge has joined the so-called "war on science," and serves to help keep the root cause of change (imagination) in check, for the sake of social stability, and to allow for direction and oversight, ... for everyone's convenience.

Information creation tends to produce market and other interest "bubbles." Those who first spot the next "bubble" can position themselves to reap the rewards; therefore, "bubble spotting" has become a favorite pastime,
. . . for your convenience.

If you ask three different people you will
get three different answers:
you *are* in a bubble,
you are *not* in a bubble,
and you are in a *different* bubble,
. . . for your convenience.

This page is on a word diet, and is therefore almost-blank.

6

Almost-Healthy

Information Gone Almost-Wild

It used to be that you were presumed healthy until you were diagnosed with an illness. "How are you?" "Fine."
Today, everyone knows that everyone else is afflicted with something, even if it's only partially clogged arteries, a half-baked liver, gall stones, indoor air, second-hand smoke, first-hand pesticides, mercury poisoning from your fillings and the fish you eat, food packaging extractables and leachables, cumulative exposure to cosmic radiation (especially from plane travel), at least the beginnings of carpal tunnel syndrome, insufficient exercise, stress disorders, vitamin deficiencies, less than perfect vision, gingivitis, halitosis, insomnia, deficient recall, a dated fashion sense, bad manners, poor diction, and worse genes,
and they are only too eager to help, especially with your obvious need for more and better information,
... for your convenience.

> The way to improve the health
> and healthcare of everyone is:
> to increase the amount of information
> everywhere about everyone's health,
> ... for everyone's convenience.

Information Gone Almost-Wild

The way to best guard against ill-health is to
have all your genes sequenced,
so that we can determine precisely where
you fit in the human "family tree,"
and accurately predict your chances of
getting every single disease,
and (combined with your demographic and
lifestyle information) your proclivity toward
every known calamity,
. . . for your convenience.

Almost-medicine, *n.* "Quack medicine" involving questionable diagnoses and counterfeit pharmaceuticals.

Almost-surgery, *n.* "Garage surgery" performed with inferior equipment and procedures.

Each new medication comes with information about precautions and side effects, and it would be wise to only take the medication if the benefits are going to outweigh the negatives,
... for your convenience.

Each new test and scanning device comes with information about precautions and side effects, and it would be wise to only go through with the test when the benefits are going to outweigh the negatives,
... for your convenience.

The healthier the healthcare systems
stay, the healthier everyone will be,
. . . for everyone's convenience.

Being nice to people, and being
careful in what you do and say,
are two good ways to remain
almost-healthy,
. . . for your convenience.

Eating healthy, and exercising,
are two more good ways to
remain almost-healthy,
. . . for your convenience.

This is here as an almost-blank page,
. . . for your convenience.

Mostly Helpful

Software is written for your convenience,
and for the convenience of all of the other
"stakeholders,"
. . . for your convenience.

The more *some* software developers stray
from legal and ethical behavior, the more
legal and ethical training the *other* software
developers must endure,
. . . for your convenience.

Software is often developed iteratively,
which means it gets better and more
helpful over time,
. . . for your convenience.

Not everyone is in the game for the long-term,
and some "actors" are here and gone in
microseconds.

Many previously mechanical, electrical, or
electronic equipment controls have now been
enhanced to include software intermediation,
. . . for your convenience.

Just about everything now comes with
a built-in, software-controlled
camera and microphone (eye and ear) combo,
. . . for your convenience.

It used to be that when you were on the phone you could not be interrupted because you were "busy," and when you were "out" living your life you also missed the call; but now they've fixed that (with new features, more gadgets, and more portability),
. . . for your convenience.

Downside: Now it's almost-rude when you don't succumb to every interruption.

Upside: Who doesn't want to be involved, informed, and popular!

The "help" feature is never helpful,
the manual is nowhere to be found,
and the Help Desk has just been automated
(for your convenience),
but the sad part is that you just encountered
a problem that is unique to your situation
(combination of hardware and software),
... so unfortunately you are on your own.

But we would like to copy "some files" off
your computer "so we can improve our
software later on,"
... for your convenience.

To set up a conference call
with everyone in the world,
just click here,
or call Tech Support,
and find out how easy it is to do,
. . . for your convenience.

Information Gone Almost-Wild

> The more steps you have to go
> through to get something done,
> the more ways there are for
> someone to track your progress,
> ... for your convenience.

> Nothing is as convenient or easy as it
> should be, because so many steps have
> been added to otherwise simple
> processes,
> ... for their convenience,
> ... for your convenience.

Your information can easily morph into "research information," thereby giving it a much longer "shelf" almost-life, ... for everyone's eventual convenience.

Software is moving from working "at your command," to working "on your behalf,"
. . . for your convenience.

More and more "self-awareness" is being programmed into computers (detection of when things are going wrong, or when resources are misallocated), so that we don't need to help them help us quite so much,
. . . for everyone's convenience.

The more things around you that
"just happen" on your behalf,
the more you will be pleasantly surprised,
and take that for granted,
and the more you will be able to
concentrate on your ever-more-complex
and difficult and non-automatable job,
... for your convenience.

> The better computers are at
> understanding speech and at speaking,
> the less we will need to interface with
> them in the more awkward ways,
> ... for everyone's convenience.

> The better computers are at understanding
> speech and at speaking, the more they can
> just talk to each other, and stop bothering
> everyone with their beeps and prompts,
> ... for everyone's convenience.

The better computers are at understanding speech and at speaking, the less everyone will need to rely on those imprecise, glib, inconsistent, over-emotional, diurnal humans to speak,
. . . for everyone's convenience.

In the kitchen you think about food.
When in the car, you think about places.
When you're at work you think about
business. And all the time you think
about people and ideas.

As more activities also involve the
Internet, all of the aspects of your life will
start to merge,
and comingle with everyone else's life,
which should facilitate and help in so
many ways,
. . . for your convenience.

It would be helpful if everyone would just
lead, follow, or get out of the way;
but unfortunately, while doing that,
everyone still stays *in* the way (wherever
they are in the process, and just hopes for
an ever-better status quo),
. . . for their convenience.

Information Gone Almost-Wild

Anyone can do an online query and get the "low down" on anyone else.

Some people can get a report on who is inquiring about whom.

Some people can get a report on who is inquiring about those who inquire about those who inquire about those who inquire about those who inquire about others. And so on.

Whoever you are, of course, your profile on who you've inquired about, and what inquiring about the inquiring of others you have done will need to be reviewed at some point,
. . . for your convenience.

People change, so monitoring will need
to be done more and more often,
. . . for everyone's convenience.

Information Gone Almost-Wild

What everyone is after is influence. The Institute for Propaganda Analysis is best-known for educating the public (in 1937) about seven basic propaganda devices: Name-Calling, Glittering Generality, Transfer, Testimonial, Plain Folks, Card Stacking, and Band Wagon. Advertisers have since come up with other ways to steer a herd: Avante Garde, Snob Appeal, Magic Ingredients, Wit and Humor, Facts and Figures, etc. The admonitions are usually that people need to think critically for themselves about what's in their own best interest. This has more or less sufficed, until now.

The We-Know-Exactly-What-You-Need
(WeKEWYN) approach bypasses all that
questionable, blanket and untargeted
"social engineering." Now, we have all the
facts you do, and then some, so it would
make sense that we try to help,
. . . for your convenience.

You can "opt out" all you want,
but you can never leave.

* * *

Selecting "do not track" and using
"anonymity networks" might invite *more*
interest behind the scenes, not less, and they
will certainly not let you accidentally turn
off anything important,
. . . for your convenience.

An economy built mostly on the ability to
convince people to change brands
might prove just as engaging as one
where everyone punches buttons and reads,
just as reliable as one based on moving
goods willy-nilly from place to place,
just as lively as the selective nurturing of
favorite species for food,
and just as satisfactory as attrition warfare.

1967: Turn on, tune in, drop out.

2007: Log on, find tunes, droop head.

You say "potato," I say "food fight."

8

Almost-War

Information Age warfare is all about information. Power moves through information channels, and diplomatic channels. Soldiers are trained. Both fear and optimism are conveyed. In cyber war, databases, devices, weapon systems, and command and control facilities get used and targeted, including: communication channels (and the supporting power grid), reconnaissance systems, and positioning systems. The terrorist's primary objective is to make a statement, by creating a news event.

The best way to fight a war is
either with information,
or with the lack of information,
for "their convenience,"
. . . for your convenience.

Wars are won and lost with
information—who has what
information, and when.

Almost-war, *n.* When weapons became too powerful, all-out war became "mutually assured destruction" (or MAD), and we had to learn to fight the "almost-way." Almost-war has become the almost-norm now (in many arenas). Almost-war can be described as any serious dispute other than all-out war, especially a lukewarm or halfhearted war.
- from *The Almost-Dictionary.*

It used to be whose army won that was important, now it's whose narrative wins that is most important,
. . . for everyone's convenience.

Don't publish anything you don't want the enemy/competition to know.

You need at least a mostly-informed electorate and public to maintain a viable democracy.

The best way to spy on
another country
is to exchange information with
the other country.

Incidentally, this is also the best
way to make friends with that
other country.

(Or person, or company, or
world, . . . partner.)

> The way to fight an idea is with another better alternative idea.

> It's becoming harder to tell the good ideas from the bad ones, because now they all grow in the same large global incubator.

Beware of the ideas behind the ideas,
that perhaps only seem to be on your side,
and for your convenience,
. . . for your convenience.

The easiest way to make all of the equipment in another country fail at the same time is to first become the manufacturer of all of the equipment in that country, and then, later, to make it all fail at the same time,
. . . for your convenience.

Caveat emptor.

For every action in war, the unequal and not-necessarily-opposite reaction can be wildly unpredictable, and is usually timed for *their* convenience.

This almost-blank page is over here.

9

Almost-There

101 Reasons to Not Use Cash:

- you could be given the wrong change by accident
- bills are flammable
- it's hard to tell if you have just been given a counterfeit bill
- the pictures on the currency are always sooo "last week"
- change can wear a hole in your pocket
- change can jingle and annoy
- change weighs too much
- sorting bills and change wastes time
- you need to keep going back to the bank for more
- if you get asked for "spare change," you can always truthfully say you don't have any
- it's easier to record and organize your transactions if they are digital from the outset (the more money is like other information the better)
- multi-system receipts make for better alibis
- you can impress your friends with the amount you can spend on credit
- the more information the authorities can get automatically, the less they will require from you later
- you will never need to estimate, and then later find out that your estimate was way off

Progress that is steady and gradual is
usually the safest and most desirable,
. . . for everyone's convenience.

Progress tends to happen
in fits and starts.

Information Gone Almost-Wild

> In the future,
> Clark Gable and Vivien Leigh
> will be able to star in any movie
> of your choosing,
> ... for your convenience.

> In the future,
> you
> will be able to star in any
> movie of your choosing,
> ... for your convenience.

In the future, the distinction between each "virtual" reality and the realities around it will blur,
. . . for your convenience.

In the future, the job of correcting
erroneous information
will be done automatically,
accurately or otherwise,
... for everyone's patient convenience.

In the future, the job of correcting
erroneous information
will still be done manually,
by exceedingly trustworthy employees,
accurately or otherwise,
... for everyone's patient convenience.

(As identity proofing becomes ever more elaborate.)

The more erroneous information that is not
corrected, the more accidents, or "accidents,"
will happen because of erroneous information.

The more information, the more information
that will need to be maintained,
. . . for everyone's convenience.

In the future, a quasi-official version of history may emerge (a database that includes a copy of all books, etc., ever written) for easy searches (and maybe for a few easy, helpful and normalizing "find and replace" edits), ... for everyone's convenience.

> In the future, there will be laws regulating how quickly history may be modified,
> ... for everyone's convenience.

New movie just out:
Gone With The Information
starring Clarke Gable, Vivien Leigh, and You,
... for your convenience.

Frankly my dear, I forgot what I was going to say.

In the future, you may need to spend more for defense (information security, privacy, and reputation protection) than you will for offence (new advantage-giving information), and the organizations that provide one service are well-positioned to provide the other,
... for your convenience.

* * *

(Nobody *doesn't* want to be an information provider.)

> Any organization with a database
> already has built-in costs for
> information security and privacy, and
> maintaining data integrity,
> you just aren't being charged for those
> things separately yet,
> ... for your convenience.

> In the future, there will be
> at least one new way of socializing
> invented every day,
> ... for your convenience.

> In the future, there will be
> at least one new way of socializing
> made illegal every day,
> ... for your convenience.

Your *auto*biography is being written
*auto*matically as we speak,
and anything you say or do to influence the
outcome of the narrative will be duly noted,
. . . for your convenience.

If you still choose to write a version
of your *auto*biography your*self*,
that will also be included for the record,
. . . for your convenience.

In the future, there could be
a fake fly on every wall, and a fake
dragonfly following everyone around,
. . . for your protection and convenience.

In the future, almost-all "surveillance"
will be surveillance equipment spying
on other surveillance equipment,
. . . for your convenience.

(Because the amount of surveillance
equipment will be growing at a much
faster rate than the human
population, and also because as
surveillance equipment gets smarter
there will be a greater need for it to be
monitored.)

> If there is such a thing as people stifling their own behaviors because they are being monitored, then the new "almost-normal" we are moving toward might be "social almost-paralysis."

There's a satellite for everything.

If there isn't a satellite for it yet, there will be.

> The faster everything moves,
> the shorter reaction times will become,
> and the more likely the simple procedure
> "Ready, Aim, Fire,"
> will become
> "Ready, Fire, Aim,"
> or "Fire, Fire, Fire,"
> or "Almost-Ready, Not Ready."

> Of course it's worth doing,
> but it would take so long that
> we would be overtaken by events.

It is already possible for those with a "need-to-know" to see through the thin veil of anonymity everywhere.
Gradually we all will be able to know everything about the people we meet—on the street, indoors, and online.

In the future, "non-actors" just living their lives will be winning most of the acting awards.
(Perhaps, the "Almost-Oscars.")

In the future, you will only be able to get your "15 minutes of privacy" when you visit one of those special bunker-style pay-toilets.

Information Gone Almost-Wild

In the future, your insurance premiums and other risk-based numbers will real-time auto-adjust as your personal habits and surrounding conditions change,
. . . for your convenience.

In the future, everything will have a reliable lie detection feature,
and will also be able to rate speech with respect to euphemism boldness, metaphor appropriateness, sleaze factor, directness, accent, cliché usage, and originality of content.

In the future, we will find out how much "like" and "love" and "respect" are really correlated with NOT knowing everything about the other person.

In the future, people will need to pretend they don't know things about each other, just so they can engage in what we today call "casual personal conversations."

In the future, doors are going to
open and close for you in surprising
ways as more and more people
have access to influence your life,
. . . for your convenience.

If at first you don't succeed,
give up, relax, and look around for
your paths of least resistance.

> In the future, much more information-gathering will be done from inside the human body.

Information-related psychological problems already abound (stress, anxiety, insomnia, nightmares, depression, and some phobias, and psychosomatic illnesses). New disorders are likely to emerge that might make this department even more interesting. To start, perhaps: "rollingstop stigmatitis," "permanent embarrassment," "chronic stage-fright," "chipinheadalgia," and "billionfriendiasis of the spleen."

In the future, there will be many new ways to
control the flow of information,
. . . for your convenience.

Information may want to be free,
but much of it needs to be only almost-free.
("Free-range," or inexpensive.)

In the future, the surface of
almost everything will be an
ever-changing billboard,
. . . for your convenience.

In the future, we will all need to change our minds at the same time.

No, you first.

In the future, the job of disabling automatics and de-programming things will be ever-more difficult and increasingly specialized, as we progress and evolve in new ways,
. . . for your convenience.

If society collapses, it still could be for a lack of information, but it might also be because mostly-free and energized information (memes) will not tolerate restraint, and everything and everybody has gotten so much smarter and self-reliant that the forces that bind just may not be strong enough anymore,
. . . for your convenience.

> Of course, by the time we actually get to the future, it will have changed, ... for your convenience.

Almost-Somebody

> Our world is in a delicate near-equilibrium, and significant changes to it potentially threaten everyone.

> Our world is robust and resilient, and an ever-evolving testing ground for new possibilities,
> ... for everyone's convenience.

Everything is being reoriented
to work globally,
. . . for everyone's convenience.

Regional differences are what
lend competitive advantage,
. . . for everyone's convenience.

When it takes only one "bad apple" to ruin things for everyone in not just a village anymore but a "global village," many "possible opportunity" paths will be blocked, or never explored in the first place, . . . for everyone's convenience.

Science fiction continues to point to where we might go off track, so that we can avoid the pitfalls, . . . for everyone's convenience.

> Currently, our wars are on crime, drugs, terrorism, obesity, inflation, pollution, high energy prices, poverty, stupidity, and visible panty lines (VPL). It's like war wants to be against bad ideas, not groups of people.

> Our world is actively avoiding pathologies, ... for everyone's convenience.

Information Gone Almost-Wild

> The structures are in place whereby "world thinking" can be managed (governed) through the various media in a concerted way,
> ... for everyone's convenience.
>
> The structures are in place whereby the world "blood supply" (money) can flow everywhere,
> ... for everyone's convenience.
>
> The structures are in place whereby ideas can get everywhere instantly (phones, the Internet, satellites, software-enabled cameras, microphones, and displays),
> ... for everyone's convenience.

The world financial markets consist of both the information processing performed by computers, and the neural processing of information done by humans.

Societies today consist of both the information processing performed by computers, and the neural processing of information done by humans.

Computers and people both gather, process, and pass on information, thereby keeping the markets and societies alive.

> To the world, everything in it is both
> a resource and a risk.
> (That's a "body" for you.)

> Information processing is what
> a brain does, and it is also what
> a world does,
> ... for everyone's convenience.

The Information Age is our world's
way of keeping an eye on everyone,
. . . for everyone's convenience,
. . . for the world's convenience.

The Information Age is
happening because the world is
trying to make up its own mind
about everything.

Our world is a "brain of brains," it has been ever since biological evolution began, and with creative evolutionary improvements it is gaining in power daily, ... for everyone's convenience.

"Global thinking" is becoming Almost-Somebody.

Like a brain of neurons, the global "brain of brains" has purpose, drive, ambition, personality, self-control, patience, impatience, perseverance, and it develops and follows rules of behavior. It deserves rights. It is to some extent self-healing, and self-correcting,
... for everyone's convenience.

Each "brain of brains" (group or society) acts brain-like *to some degree*: a tight network may depend more on groupthink, interdependency, and teamwork, whereas a network of loose and distant associations is more inclined toward self-sufficiency and independent thinking.

Information Gone Almost-Wild

Abraham Maslow's "hierarchy of needs" for humans can be tweaked to produce one for worlds:

Self-actualization: Our world is trying to be all that it can be: it is exploring its own interests, steering its own thinking, and being creative.
Esteem: Our world hasn't found another world to impress yet, but it still needs to impress people generally, and it knows what the criteria are.
Belonging: Our world is currently looking for other worlds, especially ones that are similar.
Safety: What is bad for a world is usually also bad for its inhabitants, so our world has many defenders. Collisions with other galactic bodies, radiation, cold, and isolation, are all safety issues.
Basic needs: Food (energy), shelter (a magnetosphere), a phone (radio telescopes), and basic cable (a technosphere), together make for a good start.

Even if there isn't another world to compare our world to yet, it can be tentatively rated on the "Big Five" personality traits (OCEAN):

Openness:
inventive/curious vs. consistent/cautious.
Conscientiousness:
efficient/organized vs. easy going/careless.
Extraversion:
outgoing/energetic vs. solitary/reserved.
Agreeableness:
friendly/compassionate vs. cold/unkind.
Neuroticism:
sensitive/nervous vs. secure/confident.

Our world needs people:
a) as technicians to develop the proper structures and supports, and
b) as teachers to properly guide it.

As we know from biology, an amazing mind doesn't survive and thrive without an amazing body.

In an emergent evolution, new things and ways emerge, and the times ahead will probably be as turbulent and engaging as ever, . . . for everyone's convenience.

Information Gone Almost-Wild

> Worlds are born, and they die. Our world (Earth) was born about 4.5 billion years ago, and it is doomed to be engulfed by our then red giant Sun in just over 5 billion years from now.
>
> According to estimates though, it will cease to be suitable for human habitation long before that (probably before 1 billion years from now),
> for everyone's inconvenience.

> Worlds eventually want to find other worlds, and to make baby worlds,
> . . . for everyone's convenience.

Just like there are harmonies and
disharmonies in a person's thinking, so
there will continue to be harmonies and
disharmonies in the world's thinking,
. . . for your convenience.

Information doesn't make the
world go 'round,
but information does help the
world grow up.

Our world is partly beautiful and partly ugly, partly strong and partly weak, partly rigid and partly flexible, partly informed and partly under-informed, partly proud and partly humble, partly right and partly wrong, partly honest and partly deceitful, partly caring and partly selfish, partly confident and partly unsure, partly open and partly private, partly hopeful and partly despairing, partly hostile and partly peaceful, partly good and partly bad, partly complex and partly simple, partly chaotic and partly organized, partly left and partly right, partly yin and partly yang, partly restrained and partly free, partly a unit and partly a multiplicity, partly alive and partly dead,
. . . just like everybody else.

More and more, our world is
learning to speak with one voice,
... for everyone's convenience.

Our world has never spoken with more
and more-different voices,
... for everyone's convenience.

This is almost the last almost-blank page.

Almost-Concluded

Almost everything now still depends on:

a) **encryption** (and other security features),

b) **cooperation** (at all levels),

c) both the flexibility and rigidity of information **use limitations**.

Both uncertainty and rapid change
seem likely to continue, as we
remain perpetually
on the edge of something wild.

Surprise! Surprise!

While you were reading this book,
the amount of information in the world has
increased prodigiously,
. . . for your convenience.

Appendices

Information Gone Almost-Wild

An almost-unnecessary almost-blank page.

Appendices

1 – More About Almost-Somebody

The Almost-Somebody perspective of planet Earth is similar to other perspectives and phrasings. I mention a few here so that it is not seen in isolation.

The Almost-Somebody perspective agrees with the ancient Gaia (Mother Earth) mythology in that Earth acts as nurturer and teacher.

The Almost-Somebody perspective is in accord with Thomas Hobbes's view of "the Commonwealth" (or State) in that the matter, form, power, and actions of the collective can be considered as that of a single entity in many ways (as expressed in his book *Leviathan*, 1651). There was a picture of a person comprised of many people representing "the society" on his original cover.

There are similarities between our world and that presented in *Gray's Anatomy* (1858), as well as most of the books on psychology. If you were to start from scratch and build a worldwide system that tries to get all the right information to all the right places at the right time, and simultaneously squeeze out miscommunication and inappropriate communication, then you would probably also say that you were building some kind of nervous system.

The Almost-Somebody idea is consistent with the observation of Sigmund Freud and others that past experience strongly influences behavior in the present. This is a world that can be analyzed, diagnosed, and educated. The vestiges of "junk DNA" thought and "old ways" are everywhere.

The Almost-Somebody concept can be considered a continuation from Pierre Teilhard de Chardin's "noosphere" concept, which is, as he put it, "the thinking envelope of the Earth," and a "super-Brain." (However, unlike the direction Chardin went in, this projection is not teleological.)

There will undoubtedly be more melding and interplay between bits and atoms, and who knows how far off or extreme the depictions in these works are: the movie *Tron* (1982), William Gibson's book *Neuromancer* (1984), and the movies: *Virtuosity* (1995), and *The Matrix* (1999).

Information Gone Almost-Wild

The science of artificial intelligence (AI) has come a long way, and is producing better and better brains—many of which outperform the human brain at some mental function now. For Almost-Somebody, super-sentience and super-consciousness may start by spreading from a part to the whole. Again, in the movies, we have seen possibilities of how this may happen in the depiction of Skynet in *The Terminator* (1984), and with the super-computer Autonomous Reconnaissance Intelligence Integration Analyst (ARIIA) in *Eagle Eye* (2008), for example.

Vernor Vinge's "technological singularity" (or "intellectual event horizon") is a point beyond which it would be hard to predict outcomes. The super-being is usually spoken of as a technologically advanced individual, not a world, but one might wonder how a super-being or beings would relate to and/or dominate the whole world. According to both Vernor Vinge and Ray Kurzweil, the technological singularity is the point where humans lose control.

That won't be the end of the world, of course. Just because one species loses the control it thinks it has, that transition doesn't *necessarily* imply that all control will be lost, or that the world will lose self-control. The smartest guy in the room becomes boss more often than he turns outlaw. The transition could happen gradually, or suddenly. The world moves in mysterious ways sometimes, and these ways are proving to be even more difficult to understand than an individual human's psychology. (These ways are studied now via the disciplines of economics and sociology, and influenced through politics, law, and business.)

Today, there is the continual removal of humans from the decision-making process: it started with the little trivial decisions, and is working its way up the scale to the ever more critical ones. Meanwhile, Nietzsche's "overman" is still out there, teasing and beckoning. Everyone wants more powers under their belt. Humans have started down the road to becoming cyborgs (with pacemakers, bionics, embedded chips, nanotechnology, and the like), for longevity and self-improvement purposes, but these transhumanist efforts might not be able to keep pace with other changes.

Only the world has "all the time in the world," but even that amount of time is limited, so Almost-Somebody has some serious thinking to do. Current estimates are that simple cells (prokaryotes) probably emerged about 3.8 billion years ago, photosynthesis about

Appendices

3 billion years ago, complex cells (eukaryotes) about 2 billion years ago, multi-cellular life about 1 billion years ago, vertebrates about 500 million years ago, and mammals about 200 million years ago. Also, it is estimated that Earth will be too hot to support liquid water in 1 billion years from now. So given that Earth has already lived and grown through more than half of its prime evolving weather, it must be circumspect and careful about decisions that could cause serious setbacks. Charles Darwin published *The Origin Of Species* a mere 152 years ago (when idea-based evolution finally definitively trumped biological evolution), and worldly capabilities are only now getting interesting.

As this exercise in spartanizing has hopefully shown, humans have a lot to think about too. That is why information awareness is the biggest issue of our age.

Information Gone Almost-Wild

An "unruly" almost-blank page.

Appendices

2 - The Laws of Info-Dynamics

Zeroth Law – If two information systems are in synch with a third, they will be in synch with one another (but only until someone makes an update to one of them, then they become "out of synch" again—which is a less-special situation).

First Law – Information can be created and destroyed. Information can also be copied easily (and/or copied with slight mutations or customizations), which is its greatest strength.

Second Law – Closed information systems *seem* to age rapidly. Open information systems tend to enlarge, tend toward greater complexity, and without proper maintenance they also tend toward disorder and chaos.

Third Law – Just by existing, information can and often does produce unintended consequences, which may in turn trigger further unintended consequences, actions, and reactions.

My paraphrasing of the Laws of Thermodynamics

Information Gone Almost-Wild

An almost-unbreakable almost-blank page.

3 - The Laws of Info-biology

First Law – The phenomena of life (and information processing) are never *in*consistent with chemistry and physics.

Second Law – The cell is the fundamental unit of life; and the object/file (information encapsulated) is the fundamental unit of information.

Third Law – Replication is the key to longevity.

Fourth Law – Information evolves.

My paraphrasing of the Laws of Biology

Information Gone Almost-Wild

These almost-blank pages are actually all quite similar.

4 - Murphy's Laws about Information

A collection:

- Anything that can go wrong, has *already* gone wrong! You just haven't been notified yet.

- If the information can get into the wrong hands, it will.

- If a message can be interpreted in several ways, it will be interpreted in a manner that maximizes the damage.

- You will always find the information you want in the last place you look.

- The best idea will arrive too late for it to be acted upon.

- You will discover an easy way to do it, after you've finished doing it.

- Field experience is something you don't get until just after you need it.

- Whenever you set out to do something, something else must be done first.

- For every action, there is an equal and opposite criticism.

- There is always someone who knows better than you what you meant with your message.

- Things get worse under pressure.

- Anyone who isn't paranoid simply isn't paying attention.

- The two most abundant things in all the universe are hydrogen and stupidity.

- It is impossible to make anything foolproof, because fools are so ingenious.

- When in doubt, mumble. When in trouble, delegate. When the idea is only half-baked, make it sound convincing.

- Nothing is impossible for the person who doesn't have to do it themselves.

- Every rule has an exception, including this rule.

- If you do assume Murphy's Law is working in a particular case, that will be the one time when it doesn't apply.

Appendices

5 - Almost-Quoted Almost-Above

The following quotes are mentioned, rephrased, or alluded to in the previous pages:

A spectre is haunting Europe – the spectre of Communism.
- **Karl Marx and Friedrich Engels** (*The Communist Manifesto*, 1848)

In this sense, the theory of the Communists may be summed up in this single sentence: Abolition of private property.
- **Karl Marx and Friedrich Engels** (*The Communist Manifesto*, 1848)

All animals are equal, but some animals are more equal than others.
- **George Orwell** (*Animal Farm*, 1945)

You can check-out any time you like, but you can never leave!
- **Eagles** (*Hotel California*, 1976)

Turn on, tune in, drop out.
- **Timothy Leary (and Marshall McLuhan)**

Information wants to be free.
- **Stewart Brand**

In the future, everyone will be world-famous for 15 minutes.
- **Andy Warhol**

Man is a rope, tied between beast and overman — a rope over an abyss.
 - **Friedrich Nietzsche** (*Thus Spoke Zarathustra*, 1883-1885)

Information Gone Almost-Wild

This page is only "almost-blank."

Appendices

6 - Other Related Quotes

The following quotes are included because they relate to the various subjects covered in the previous pages:

If a man neglects education, he walks lame to the end of his life.
- **Plato**

The more you know, the more you know you don't know.
- **Aristotle**

Supply creates its own demand.
- **Jean Baptiste Say** (known as Say's Law)

As a general rule, the most successful man in life is the man who has the best information.
- **Benjamin Disraeli**

It is a very sad thing that nowadays there is so little useless information.
- **Oscar Wilde**

There is only one thing in the world worse than being talked about, and that is not being talked about.
- **Oscar Wilde**

Everybody is ignorant, only on different subjects.
- **Will Rogers**

Nine-tenths of wisdom is being wise in time.
- **Theodore Roosevelt**

Every reform movement has a lunatic fringe.
- **Theodore Roosevelt**

The only thing we have to fear is fear itself.
- **Franklin D. Roosevelt**

Every sentence that I utter must be understood not as an affirmation, but as a question.
- **Niels Bohr**

Everything should be made as simple as possible, but not simpler.
- **Albert Einstein**

Science may be described as the art of systematic over-simplification—the art of discerning what we may with advantage omit.
- **Karl Popper**

I like restraint, if it doesn't go too far.
- **Mae West**

You can't have a lasting civilization without plenty of pleasant vices.
- **Aldous Huxley**

Sixty-two thousand four hundred repetitions make one truth.
- **Aldous Huxley**

Brawndo's got what plants crave. It's got electrolytes.
- **Movie:** *Idiocracy* (2006)

The past is never dead. It's not even past.
- **William Faulkner**

History is hard to know, because of all the hired bullshit.
- **Hunter S. Thompson**

Who controls the past controls the future: who controls the present controls the past.
- **George Orwell**

The decision to reject one paradigm is always simultaneously the decision to accept another, and the judgment leading to that decision involves the comparison of both paradigms with nature *and* with each other.
- **Thomas S. Kuhn**

Appendices

Doublethink means the power of holding two contradictory beliefs in one's mind simultaneously, and accepting both of them.
- **George Orwell**

May we never confuse honest dissent with disloyal subversion.
- **Dwight D. Eisenhower**

A man who limits his interests, limits his life.
- **Vincent Price**

It's a small world after all.
- **The Sherman Brothers** (for Walt Disney)

The medium is the message.
- **Marshall McLuhan**

Reality leaves a lot to the imagination.
- **John Lennon**

Without deviation from the norm, progress is impossible.
- **Frank Zappa**

The best way to predict the future is to create it.
- **Peter Drucker**

The ultimate censorship is the flick of the dial.
- **Tommy Smothers**

Any sufficiently advanced technology is indistinguishable from magic.
- **Arthur C. Clarke**

Perspective is worth 80 IQ points.
- **Alan Kay**

Minds are what brains do.
- **Marvin Minsky**

They say the world has become too complex for simple answers.
They are wrong.
- **Ronald Reagan**

If there are any complaints that you'd like to make, I'd be only too happy to send you the appropriate forms.
- **Movie:** *Brazil* (1985)

Within thirty years, we will have the technological means to create superhuman intelligence. Shortly thereafter, the human era will be ended.
- **Vernor Vinge** (1993)

If computers get too powerful, we could organize them into a committee—that would do them in.
- **Bradley's Bromide**

The meme for blind faith secures its own perpetuation by the simple unconscious expedient of discouraging rational inquiry.
- **Richard Dawkins**

Darwinism is now seen to be the survival of the survivors at the level of pure, digital code.
- **Richard Dawkins**

There is an unacceptably large gap between the world that could be and the world that currently is, but it is the power of ideas that will cross that gap.
- **Newt Gingrich**

Words are the new weapons, satellites are the new artillery.
- **Bond Movie:** *Tomorrow Never Dies* (1997)

Don't look up.
- **Movie:** *Enemy of the State* (1998)

The final frontier is not space, it is the human imagination.
- **Boeing, Inc.** (television advertisement, 2002)

Appendices

The information encoded in your DNA determines your unique biological characteristics, such as sex, eye color, age and Social Security number.
- **Dave Barry**

The nature of an innovation is that it will arise at a fringe where it can afford to become prevalent enough to establish its usefulness without being overwhelmed by the inertia of the orthodox system.
- **Kevin Kelly**

Healthcare is going through a period of amalgamating into larger and larger systems.
- **Kevin Kelly**

File sharing is killing the artistic middle-class.
- **Jaron Lanier**

Sometimes the very things we put in place to safeguard our liberty, become threats to liberty themselves.
- **Movie:** *Eagle Eye* (2008)

The biggest challenge the world faces is information security.
- **David DeWalt** (CEO, McAfee, Inc.)

Maybe we should amend Adam Smith's trademark metaphor of the invisible hand. ... Hand's aren't very cerebral, after all; guiding any invisible hand must be an "invisible brain." It's neurons are people.
- **Robert Wright**

If the world was perfect, it wouldn't be.
- **Yogi Berra**

As intelligence saturates the matter and energy available to it, it turns dumb matter into smart matter.
- **Ray Kurzweil**

Information Gone Almost-Wild

The Edge. . . . There is no honest way to explain it because the only people who really know where it is are the ones who have gone over.
- Hunter S. Thompson

When the going gets weird, the weird turn pro.
- Hunter S. Thompson

Don't panic.
- Douglas Adams

Information Gone Almost-Wild

. . . and so the hopeful quest for more and better and faster information continues,
. . . for your convenience.

Information Gone Almost-Wild

www.ingramcontent.com/pod-product-compliance
Lightning Source LLC
Chambersburg PA
CBHW061429040426
42450CB00007B/968